SILVER SERIES OF GROWN-UP WISDOM

HERBERT HATRED

Janet Snyder and Kathleen Canova

Published by
Hasmark Publishing International
www.hasmarkpublishing.com

Copyright © 2024 Janet Snyder & Kathleen Canova

First Edition

No part of this book may be reproduced or transmitted in any form or by any means, electronic or mechanical, including photocopying, recording or by any information storage and retrieval system, without written permission from the author, except for the inclusion of brief quotations in a review.

Disclaimer:
This book is designed to provide information and motivation to our readers. It is sold with the understanding that the publisher is not engaged to render any type of psychological, legal, or any other kind of professional advice. The content of each article is the sole expression and opinion of its author, and not necessarily that of the publisher. No warranties or guarantees are expressed or implied by the publisher's choice to include any of the content in this volume. Neither the publisher nor the individual author(s) shall be liable for any physical, psychological, emotional, financial, or commercial damages, including, but not limited to, special, incidental, consequential or other damages. Our views and rights are the same: You are responsible for your own choices, actions, and results.

Permission should be addressed in writing to Janet & Kathy at janet@storybookpath.com.

Cover Design: Anne Karklins [anne@hasmarkpublishing.com]
Interior Layout: Amit Dey [amit@hasmarkpublishing.com]
Illustrations: Believer

ISBN 13: 978-1-77482-303-3
ISBN 10: 1-77482-303-9

Dedication

We dedicate this book to **"We the People."**

With knowledge, growth, and wisdom gained through crafting this story, we were reminded of the phrase, "life, liberty, and the pursuit of happiness" which appears in the United States Declaration of Independence.

Life is meant to be fun and joyful.

Liberty is actually something that comes from within each of us.

Joy is a human emotion we can attain. Happiness "comes and goes" but Joy is a condition.

Joy, Knowledge, Empowerment, Freedom, Love, and Appreciation are all human emotions for our mature development. Hatred, Rage, Fear, Grief, Despair and Revenge are opposing emotions. It is each individual's choice, a duty, to climb onward and upward to a fulfilling life filled with JOY!

With appreciation, we dedicate this book to the talented illustrator, Believer.

With no direction from us, his interpretation and art tells a story within our story. While we are oceans apart, Believer understands the fragility of a nation.

Acknowledgements

In gratitude for the unconditional love, encouragement, and support we've received from our **families** ~ those we were born into as well as those we helped create.

In gratitude for our dear **friends** who've been on this writing journey with us, especially those who have continued to coax and cheer us onward for years.

In gratitude for our brilliant **behind-the-scene creative duo**, Kimberly Lauersdorf and Kristan Clark, with candid critiques, enthusiastic readings, and challenging prep-talks.

In gratitude for the **crowd-funding** opportunity through BackerKit, and especially Lafia Morrow's leadership, laughter and navigation of this innovative financial pathway.

In gratitude for the **co-publishing** partnership with Hasmark Publishing International, especially its Founder, Judy O'Beirn's personal buy-in of this project and Jenn Gibson's capable leadership and coordination of their talented team.

In gratitude for the **lived experiences** we write about, because life is definitely not a spectator's sport; and we're proudly battle-tested warriors, now stronger, wiser and more compassionate having traveled these roads.

In gratitude for the **faith and freedom** to be true to ourselves, willing to tell bold stories, the good, the bad and the ugly; truly a legacy project for our culturally-relevant times.

In gratitude to **The Maker of Heaven and Earth, The Divine One** who introduced us to each other as teenagers, so that we could ultimately fulfill our life's purpose these many decades later, creating works of art and entertainment that will inspire humans forever.

In gratitude of our banner, **Silver Series of Grown-Up Wisdom**, a divine gift that we hold sacred, as we commit to creating and nurturing a genre of those "becoming" and "being" grown-up. It has been said, "it takes a village" to raise a child; and we believe that holds true when raising up "big kids" too. May our thought-provoking, illustrated short stories for grown-ups warm the hearts and minds of our beloved readers, and flourish for many generations.

T he first and most important thing you must understand regarding *Herbert* is ... he doesn't give **two shits** about you or me—**and that's a shocking fact for a leader of a large nation.**

Herbert Rhetoric Hatred got elected as Commander-in-Chief in an extremely close election; and perhaps it's true that he got a little help from a foreign power! In his new role, he often displayed a consistent pattern of grandiosity, coupled with a vindictive nature, traits commonly associated with Narcissistic Personality Disorder (NPD).

From the commencement of his term in office, and not deterred by laws, the new ringleader sought every opportunity for his administration to work in his personal favor and on his behalf. As a businessman who was accustomed to shady business dealings before becoming Commander, this was now a part of the new playbook at his Official Residence and workplace.

Many staffers either got on board with his playbook, or they didn't last long in this administration. But he clearly didn't act alone, as he demanded loyalty while manipulating many of his top people to join in as they weaponized governmental departments and employees to do their bidding. Not even batting an eye, they seemed to commit crimes without giving it a second thought.

This Commander *LOVED* his **powerful** new position. He loved it so much that he decided that he would *NEVER* give it up!

However, in this nation, presidents are elected during a general election which occurs every four years. And, according to the Constitution, there's a limit on how many times a person can be elected to the presidency … and that's twice!

Early on in this new regime of leadership, it became obvious to many citizens that we were now living in truly unprecedented times. Oftentimes, perplexed and dismayed, people everywhere did not quite know how to contend with this new chief, who clearly disrespected laws, procedures, and the generally-accepted guardrails of the country's democracy.

While many took comfort and solace in the fact that the founders had, many centuries ago, established distinct branches of government, each with its own vested power granted to the Commander, the Assembly, and the Unionized Courts, others worried it wouldn't matter with a corrupt administration in control. It seemed clear that systems were failing!

This became so disconcerting that many people began to speak out! Former colleagues, business associates, and even some family members of the Commander went public. Some even published books about Herbert's early childhood mental and emotional traumas, his inappropriate personal life escapades (especially during his adulthood), and his long career of many disastrous and failed business endeavors.

Trained mental health experts began educating the people about the serious consequences of this toxic blend of adverse childhood experiences (ACEs), combined with his dysfunctional, enabled, privileged lifestyle, and the dangerous impact from his primary role model having been a white supremacist father.

At minimum, it became clear we were dealing with a true con man who wielded hatred upon many. Some began to surmise it was even worse than that. People on both sides of the political divide questioned his "sound mind," but most importantly, people felt at a loss as to what could we do now?!

Meanwhile, this Commander saw himself as **THE** most powerful man in the free world, a wealthy,

star-powered celebrity of sorts, now using his manipulative, charismatic personality to create a cult following of fans.

Having split the political party that helped him get elected, he contorted and twisted the meanings of "Patriotism" and "Christianity." His base of followers bought his lies, disinformation, misinformation, and conspiracies. Many found themselves deeply embedded in his cult following, where it seemed easier to blame others for all the inadequacies, injustices, and imperfections of everyday life!

This president's playbook tactics were filled with his ramped-up rhetorical rants, deep-seated anger, rage, and evil hatred. He was masterful at riling it up, stoking it, fueling it through repetition, and using it to advance his own personal desire to be the *"Boss of all of us, forever."*

Herbert, the new ringleader, extremely self-absorbed, a masterful liar, and compassionless, with a sadistic personality, embodied hatred.

Just like every other wannabe dictator, Herbert Hatred invaded our sensibilities and focused on who he could hurt the most—women and minorities. Daily, he paints foreigners and immigrants as potential threats. Herbert Hatred challenges women's social status, undermining gender equality and interfering with laws protecting women's reproductive rights.

Let's pause for a moment to reflect on "hatred," a reaction to some form of inner pain, usually stemming from fear, insecurity, or mistrust. It's an attitude that can give rise to hostility and aggression toward individuals or groups.

Hatred is driven by two key emotions: "love" and "aggression." On the one hand, it feels "love for the 'in' group." On the other hand, it has "aggression for the 'out' group."

Generally, the group that is deemed different is referred to as the "other." One reason we experience hate is having a basic fear of things that are different from our own way of thinking or believing!

So, as the first term of this Commander was coming to an end, he ran for reelection, and from the "get-go," he began planting the poisonous seeds of doubt that the only way he couldn't win reelection would be if it was stolen.

So, when he actually did lose the general election, and also lost every court battle his lawyers fought to disprove their loss, many of his cohorts also signed on, helping spread his big lie that the election was stolen!

To magnify their message of the "big lie/stolen election," one of the major news outlets totally embraced it. And, it was clear their ravenous audience signed on too, believing that the election was actually stolen.

They maintained their high-ranking media presence—for a while, anyway. At the time, it seemed prudent for their financial bottom line as a network; this safeguarded top anchors' lucrative salaries, while satisfying their sponsors and viewers.

It's worth noting that this major news outlet settled a Defamation

Suit for over $700 million for pushing conspiracy theories that harmed a voting system company.

In addition, many lawyers seeking to hold on to power in their political party were equally complicit. So, it's not surprising that many of their followers, some not seeming to know any better, dove right down that rabbit hole of anger, hatred, and rage, believing and buying into all the rhetoric, too.

Thus began a whole new dark chapter in this glorious nation's history of what many observers and participants described as "a living hell."

We watched this cult of followers harness the hatred, channeling their negative energy, repeating and believing the rhetoric, and pledging their own personal oaths of loyalty to the defeated president.

Not willing to concede to the newly-elected president, Herbert Hatred invited his followers to our nation's beautiful architectural district as he spewed poisonous rhetoric, as if his life depended upon it, during the televised "Stop the Steal Rally." His staunch followers, gathered at the rally, fell right in line, joining forces in this misguided crusade to help him overturn the election.

On the fateful day of the rally, the defeated Commander used *power, fear, and anxiety* to stoke the crowd, letting them know they needed to "Fight; fight like HELL" and that this was now the ONLY way to save THEIR country.

Herbert Hatred was proud of the angry crowd amassed that day, knowing many had come armed with weapons that could cause much harm and destruction. He knew how easy it would be to use venom, hostility, and disgust to get them to do his bidding.

Then, the cowardly, defeated president returned to the Official Residence that would only serve as his home for a few more weeks. There he sat, alone, eyes glued to the TV for hours, waiting and watching as the mob that he invited defaced the nation's property, harming Capitol police

officers who had to resort to arm-to-arm combat tactics as the out-of-control riotous mob stormed the Capitol.

Tragically, people died as a result of the violence incited by him. Many people were arrested (and later tried and convicted, with some even being sentenced to decades in prison). Yet, many still refuse to admit he lost the election.

Fast forward to the 2024 general election, Herbert Hatred enters the race early in order to avoid indictments, and insists citizens of this glorious nation will reelect him to the Office of President once again. Now, as a convicted felon with multiple charges pending in various legal jurisdictions (indicted FOUR separate times, most trials pending), he still has millions of staunch followers! It boggles the mind.

Herbert has openly admitted that he admires Hitler, the evil dictator responsible for the Holocaust atrocities so many decades ago.

He's also infatuated with murderous autocrats and dictators around the world today. He speaks confidently about his plans to change laws and even pardon himself from the many corrupt acts that have resulted in pending indictments. He preaches, "They are coming after YOU. I am just standing in the way. I am your RETRIBUTION!"

History has taught us—far too many times—the tragic results when people remain silent in the face of overturning democracy, embracing fascism, antisemitism, intolerance, and hatred. In hindsight, it's become more obvious each day that Herbert's leadership style, through intimidation, manipulation, and control, are all strategic tools used by authoritarians. If he succeeds in winning again, he's been bold in saying he will likely banish the rule of law in this country! He will rule and reign under his **own laws**, even including banned methods of execution—"hatred breeds hatred"—and that's in his *playbook*.

Political unrest and a nation divided were well documented during the nation's Civil War

era, where families' allegiances were deeply divided and brothers fought each other. Today, 1,400+ organized hate groups and anti-government entities are creating havoc throughout this nation. We've witnessed failed governments all across the globe. Could we possibly lose this nation's democracy, too?

Hatred is like a devastating disease. It eats away at our mind and body. It's often present when we have unhealed early childhood trauma or any post-traumatic event in our lives! However, we can find building blocks to a life of hope and a better future. By making the most of yourself, you make the world a better place to live.

Give yourself permission to take a new path. All you need is the plan, the road map, and the courage to move forward.

Stop to consider for a moment: What if our weather was tied to our energy? Specifically, the energy of hatred and rage.

The Laws of the Universe teach there's a rhythm, flow, vibration, and energetic forces at work on the planet.

Every single action in the Universe produces a reaction! If the forces were hatred and rage, this would cause devastating destruction such as hurricanes and tornadoes.

Join the 30-Day,
Entry Level program for Personal Development.

We provide heartfelt, entertaining, real-life stories of adversity about the challenges of overcoming the after-effects endured from psychological and emotional childhood/young adult trauma.

Free Introductory Guidebook, '*OOOH Crap!*
WE BECOME WHAT WE THINK ABOUT'
when you sign up at
WWW.STORYBOOKPATH.COM.

Meet the Authors

Janet Snyder, is the creator of *StoryBookPath.com a 30-day personal development program* and eBook designed to help you discover and live the life you love and desire. After finding her enthusiastic, authentic voice and true strength from her own personal struggle with the negative aftereffects endured from mental and emotional childhood/young adult trauma, Janet's fulfilling her life purpose of helping others.

Also, Founder of *StoryBook Cottages*, she uses her well-earned degree for interior design and her vivacious love of the earth designing playhouses constructed from recycled materials and sustainable living green rooftops. Janet is the mother of three and a "Nan" to her grandchildren who also live in her hometown of Louisville, Kentucky.

Kathleen Canova, successful entrepreneur and founder of the Canova Group, LLC, has facilitated and educated many regarding domestic crisis intervention, including deep emotional and spiritual healing practices. Rooted from her own lived experiences, and after extensive training and certifications, she shares her heartfelt hope, passion and inspiration with humankind.

Living in Westminster, Colorado near her adult children and grandchildren, who affectionately call her "Yaya," she enjoys spending quality time with family and friends when she's not reading, writing and traveling.

Sales Page

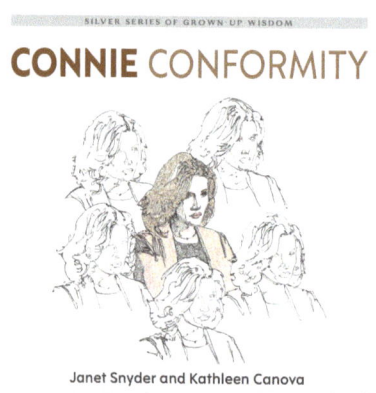
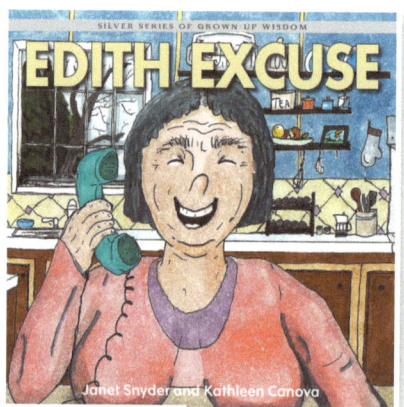

First-Time Co-Authors:

Janet Snyder and Kathleen Canova

Available on Amazon and Ingram-Spark now

www.storybookpath.com

On FACEBOOK: STORYBOOKPATH & SILVER SISTERS WISDOM

janet@storybookpath.com & kathleenkarrercanova@gmail.com